Crayfish

A Buddy Book by
Deborah Coldiron

ABDO
Publishing Company

UNDERWATER WORLD

VISIT US AT
www.abdopublishing.com

Published by ABDO Publishing Company, 8000 West 78th Street, Edina, Minnesota 55439.

Printed in the United States.

Coordinating Series Editor: Sarah Tieck
Contributing Editor: Michael P. Goecke
Graphic Design: Deborah Coldiron
Cover Photograph: U.S. Fish and Wildlife Service: Eric Engbretson
Interior Photographs/Illustrations: Animals Animals: Bill Beatty (page 13), Michael Thompson (page 17); istockphoto.com: Ilka Burckhardt (page 9), Morten Fredricksen (page 30), Kenny Haner (page 9), Jim Jurica (page 7), MBC Design Studio (page 11), Sandra O'Claire (page 29), Michael Olson (page 28), Cameron Peshak (page 27); Minden Pictures: Fred Bavendam (page 7), Fabio Liverani/NPL (page 19); PeterArnold.com: W. Poelzer/Peter Arnold Inc. (page 21), Bios Photo/Tavernier Yvette (page 21); Photos.com: (page 5, 20, 21, 23, 24, 25)

Library of Congress Cataloging-in-Publication Data

Coldiron, Deborah.
  Crayfish / Deborah Coldiron.
     p. cm. -- (Underwater world)
  Includes index.
  ISBN 978-1-60453-131-2
  1. Crayfish--Juvenile literature. I. Title.

  QL444.M33C62 2008
  595.3'84 -- dc22

                                                           2008005045

Table Of Contents

The World Of Crayfish

Every living creature needs water. Some animals not only need water, they live in it, too.

Scientists have found more than 250,000 kinds of plants and animals living underwater. And, they believe there could be one million more! The crayfish is one animal that makes its home in this underwater world.

Water covers 70 percent of Earth's surface.

Crayfish are small crustaceans (kruhs-TAY-shuhns). They are known for their powerful pinching claws.

Most adult crayfish are between two and six inches (5 and 15 cm) long. The smallest crayfish species can be less than one inch (3 cm) in length. The largest can be 16 inches (41 cm) long.

FAST FACTS

The world's largest crayfish is called the giant freshwater lobster.

Crayfish *(above)* look like smaller versions of lobsters *(below)*. Some people even call crayfish freshwater lobsters.

There are more than 500 crayfish **species**. They are found in Australia, Asia, Europe, and North America.

Most crayfish live in freshwater rivers, streams, lakes, and swamps. But, a few crayfish live in **brackish** water or salt water.

Many crayfish are brown. Others are red, green, yellow, or blue. Some are even more than one color!

A Closer Look

A crayfish's body is designed to protect it from predators. Crayfish have a tough outer shell called an exoskeleton. And, they have two large claws. The claws help crayfish defend themselves.

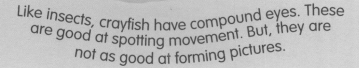

Some crayfish have brightly colored spikes on their claws.

A crayfish outgrows its exoskeleton many times. When this happens, the crayfish molts. That means it takes off its shell. Then, a new exoskeleton takes its place.

Very young crayfish molt more than once a week! Adult crayfish molt less often. The molting process leaves a crayfish tired and weak.

FAST FACTS

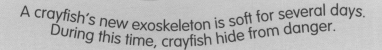

A crayfish's new exoskeleton is soft for several days. During this time, crayfish hide from danger.

Crayfish molt

Crayfish

Some crayfish eat their old exoskeletons. They contain calcium, which helps their new exoskeletons harden. Humans need calcium, too. The calcium in milk makes your bones stronger!

Crayfish have five pairs of legs for walking. They also have several shorter legs called swimmerets. These help crayfish swim.

Crayfish have eyes, but they don't see very well. Luckily, they also have antennae on their heads. These feelers help crayfish find food and protect themselves.

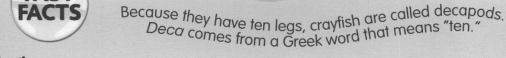
Because they have ten legs, crayfish are called decapods. Deca comes from a Greek word that means "ten."

The Body Of A Crayfish

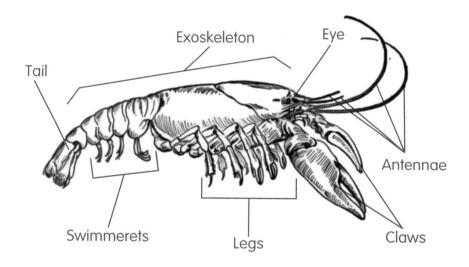

Tail

Exoskeleton

Eye

Antennae

Swimmerets

Legs

Claws

A Growing Crayfish

Crayfish often mate in autumn. But, most female crayfish wait until spring to lay their eggs.

One female crayfish can lay as many as 800 eggs at one time! She carries them with her swimmerets until they hatch. This can take 2 to 20 weeks.

FAST FACTS

When a female crayfish is holding her eggs, some people say she is "in berry." This is because the group of eggs looks like a blackberry.

Crayfish mothers are easy to catch when carrying eggs. So, they often go into hiding until the eggs hatch.

After the crayfish hatch, their mother continues holding them tightly in her swimmerets. After several weeks, they are ready to live on their own. Then, the tiny crayfish swim away.

Crayfish mothers protect their young after they hatch. But when young crayfish swim away, other animals eat some of them. Some are even eaten by other crayfish!

Family Connections

Crayfish are just one of around 42,000 known crustacean **species**. Lobsters, shrimp, and crabs are also part of this group.

All crustaceans have outer shells for protection. And, their legs and bodies are made up of small parts called segments.

The sally lightfoot crab lives near Ecuador, on the coasts of the Galápagos Islands.

Lobsters look a lot like crayfish. But, they are much larger. Some lobsters may weigh up to 100 pounds (45 kg)!

Shrimp are found in freshwater and salt water around the world.

Hermit crabs have soft bodies. So, they adopt abandoned seashells to use as houses. The seashells provide hard, strong shelters.

Dinnertime

Crayfish are nocturnal creatures. They rest and hide during the day. At night, they hunt for food.

Crayfish eat a wide variety of foods. They feed on small fish, insect larvae, and plants.

A crayfish's diet includes worms *(above)*, tadpoles *(right)*, and snails *(below)*.

A World Of Danger

A number of predators eat crayfish. Their enemies include birds, animals, and some fish.

Little blue herons and other long-legged birds wade in freshwater to find crayfish.

Sport fishermen use crayfish as bait to catch smallmouth bass and other fish.

Alligators *(above)*, turtles *(left)*, and otters *(below)* prey on crayfish.

People eat crayfish, too. For years, Louisiana's **commercial** crayfish farms have raised crayfish for eating. This protects the crayfish population in the wild.

FAST
FACTS

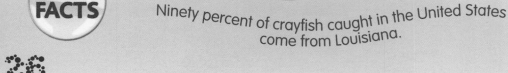

Ninety percent of crayfish caught in the United States come from Louisiana.

Some people in the southern United States catch crayfish to eat.

Fascinating Facts

🕷 If a crayfish loses a claw or a leg, it can grow another.

🕷 Crayfish are sometimes kept as pets. But beware! They eat other fish and break out of their tanks.

Crayfish live in water, so they breathe with gills. As long as their gills stay moist, crayfish can survive outside of water.

🦀 Crayfish are also known as crawfish, crawdads, and mudbugs.

🦀 Crawfish boils are a tradition in the southern United States. People fill pots of boiling water with vegetables, spices, and crayfish. Then, they serve the food on old newspapers.

Corn, lemons, onions, and potatoes are often part of a crawfish boil. People often add spicy Cajun seasonings, too.

Learn And Explore

You might think the biggest crayfish claws are the strongest. But, Indiana State University scientists disagree! Research shows that smaller claws are actually more powerful!

But, when male crayfish fight, bigger claws may still win. This is because crayfish with smaller claws often run away.

When a crayfish is trying to look tough, it raises its claws and stands tall.

IMPORTANT WORDS

brackish somewhat salty.

commercial related to business.

species living things that are very much alike.

WEB SITES

To learn more about crayfish, visit ABDO Publishing Company on the World Wide Web. Web sites about crayfish are featured on our Book Links page. These links are routinely monitored and updated to provide the most current information available.

www.abdopublishing.com

INDEX